Half a Loaf

Half A Loaf

**Johnny Bread Recipes
to Nourish the Body and Soul**

Elizabeth A. Stoltz

Photographs by Catherine R.D. Wallace

North Star Press of St. Cloud, Inc.

The St. John's Bread logo and advertisement on the back cover
used with the permission of St. John's Abbey

Copyright © 2003 Elizabeth A. Stoltz
halfaloaf03@aol.com

First Edition, January 2003

ISBN: 0-87839-195-9

Printed in the United States of America
by Versa Press, Inc., East Peoria, Illinois

Published by
North Star Press of St. Cloud, Inc.
P.O. Box 451
St. Cloud, Minnesota 56302

Fondly, for all my children
Katie, Ann, Tom, Judith, Caroline, and Meg
all of whom are good cooks

Table of Contents

Acknowledgements

Lots of people contributed to the confidence it took to write this book, confidence born from the satisfaction of many friends, students, and relatives gathered around a table again and again for many years. This book credits their influences:

+ the willingness of Bob Spaeth to come to the table to learn that food wasn't always as limited as the Army's or his mother's, and the practice and confidence it gave me—thirty years of it;
+ my children, all six of them, who grew up with a Kitchen Aid, a spoon to lick, and dishes and dishes and dishes to wash. They are my best critics;
+ especially Caroline, who willingly tested most of these recipes, with the Johnny bread going stale as it was shipped to Santa Fe;
+ all my tutors who worked for me at the St. Ben's Writing Lab/Center and loved whatever I brought them to eat—camaraderie (and philosophical conversations!) have a lot to do with food;
+ my muse, who thinks the best time to write is at 4:00 in the morning;
+ the hand of the Maker who is always at my elbow in the kitchen (for surely a rhubarb custard pie in its lattice crust hot out of the oven is indeed proof for the existence of God);
+ my grandmother, who made mashed potatoes so light they "could fly out the window," and who taught me that to feed people was to love them;
+ Jon and Gretchen, who fell in love with each other one evening right after they got up from my table;
+ Kate Wallace, for all her patience and perseverance, her talent and her skill, and all the writers who put up with my nagging to get them to write;
+ my sister-in-law, Sigrid, whose proofreading was not only thorough but perceptive as well;
+ finally my wonderful husband, Dave, who eagerly and cheerfully tasted again and again everything in this cookbook and always said it was good.

It is a wonderful thing to be able to cook, to turn the bounty we are given into something tasty and delicious. One of my students says later in this book: "Food is splendid and Johnny bread is splendid food." It's good to acknowledge what we often take for granted.

A generous pound of bread is enough for a day, whether for only one meal or for both dinner and supper. In the latter case, the cellarer will set aside one third of this pound and give it to the brothers at supper.

Rule of St. Benedict, Chapter 39

Preface

Life is full of changes: we leave our small towns, the suburbs, the big cities for a new life at college; in four years we move on to make our way in the big world; we travel to new cities, new states, new countries; we get jobs, husbands, wives, children, and then sadly we lose them. Yet we keep coming back to the place where a central part of us was formed—to our Benedictine community. And what better taste do we get when we think of that place but Johnny bread?

Johnny bread stabilized us through the late night studying and grueling exams; it could fill us up when we couldn't afford any more trips to Loso's or Linnemann's. Its familiarity connected us at Homecoming in the Old Gym, in the Great Hall, in the Palaestra shouting and drinking. We still pick up a loaf at a game or after Mass. It's there to greet us at the Johnny Stand-up reunions. Later, back home, we stand, staring out the kitchen window, drinking morning coffee or afternoon tea and eating a toasted slice with honey to recall with fondness the memories its taste evokes. It's the bread of our life.

We always take a loaf home. But how can we eat that whole huge loaf? Halfway through we stick it back into its Father Walter bag and jam it to the back of the cupboard only to find it days later getting old and hard. The loaf needs a crowd to do it justice.

So after years of crumbling up the remains and throwing them to the birds, I started to devise various ways to reuse that bread before it turned blue. What follows in this book are recipes I have concocted to use up all of that wonderful staff of life. I hope you enjoy them and the book gets you started making up your own recipes. Together we'll keep the memories alive.

Elizabeth A. Stoltz

Introduction

Here is an essential book for everyone familiar with Johnny bread—that heavy-crusted, grain-filled loaf baked in the refectory kitchen of St. John's University in Collegeville, Minnesota. I can attest to the fact that its quality hasn't varied over the past half century.

I was a student at St. John's back when it was a much different place and the students led a much more restricted existence. Today it's impossible to imagine, for example, having the lights go out at 10:30 (in Freshman dorms) or at 11:00 (upperclassmen) or being awakened for Mass at 6:30 every morning. Unthinkable, too, is a campus with no student cars allowed.

But at least three aspects of St. John's have remained constant through the years. The abbey is still an important presence on campus, the rural setting is more beautiful than ever, and Johnny bread is still as tasty as it was in the early fifties, when our waiter would set a plate of it, sliced, on our table, and if it was fresh, it would disappear in a minute; if not, there was always plenty to go around. For after its second day of existence, Johnny bread passes into its dry, hardened state and becomes difficult to chew. And that's where my friend Betty's book comes in. Here are at least thirty recipes using days-old Johnny bread in various forms:

Johnny bread slices,
Johnny bread cubes,
Johnny bread crumbs,
and Johnny bread meal.

If you are an amateur in the kitchen, as I am, you might want the difference between crumbs and meal explained to you. Crumbs are crumbs, produced by crumbling the bread as it is, whereas meal is crumbs set out to dry, then chopped up very finely in your food processor.

There is something here for every meal—breakfast, lunch, and dinner—as well as a number of delicious desserts, like chocolate chip cookies and raspberry torte. Then there are sections devoted to dorm-room snacks (including kitchen counter pizza and peanut butter Johnny bars) and specialty breads like biscotti and bruschetta. And scattered throughout the book you will find amusing reminiscences of Johnny bread from about twenty alumni, some my contemporaries, and other more recent graduates.

In trying out our latest recipe, my wife, Gretchen, prepared baked fish using Johnny bread crumbs. The Johnny bread gave the dish an unusually rich taste—it turned out to be the best tasting fish I've ever eaten. So you see, this book isn't only about putting your Johnny bread to use, it's about improving your meals as well.

Jon Hassler

Half a Loaf

Key

Each recipe in this book is keyed in the top right corner of the page according to the following three elements:

1. A degree of difficulty, indicated by *, **, or *** from simple to more complicated;
2. A category ("breakfast," "main course," etc.);
3. A number (1 to 4), which refers to the stages of stale Johnny bread used in the recipe (See page 2 for further clarification)

For example: **JB Cheesecake**   *****dessert (4)**

*** means the preparation involves a more elaborate combination of steps to get the dish ready for baking; **"dessert"** is the recipe's category, and **(4)** indicates that Johnny bread meal is used in the recipe.

Getting Ready to Use the Half a Loaf

The first half loaf of Johnny bread has been eaten—good sandwiches, good sliced bread and butter with supper, good toast and honey for breakfast. But now the other half remains. How is one to use it? The recipes in this cookbook use the bread in all of its forms: slices, cubes, crumbs, and what I call "JBmeal." The following definitions will help you determine the stages of staleness and the form the bread takes in order to prepare it for each of the recipes:

Stage 1: JBslices. I refer to slices of bread as "day-old" when the bread is no longer fresh and begins to dry out, perhaps during the first 3 or 4 days. In most of the recipes in this book that call for slices, you can leave the crusts on. But the color of the dish you are making is enhanced when the crusts are removed since the crusts are of a darker color and will change the appearance of your dish. The taste, however, will not be changed whether you leave the crusts on or take them off. Recipes call for slices of bread that are usually ½ inch to one inch thick.

Stage 2: JBcubes. Cubes of bread are cut from day-old slices. Bread pudding uses these cubes without the crusts and croutons are made from the whole slices cut into one- or two-inch squares. This is also the best form to use for stuffing.

Stage 3: JBcrumbs. Prepare the bread that is three to four days old (up to a week and then it will start to turn blue) to make bread crumbs. This can be done by pulsing about a cup at a time of torn-up bread in the food processor or by cutting or tearing the bread into small pieces, letting it dry on a cookie sheet loosely covered with plastic for a day; or by placing the cookie sheet in the oven for about 10 minutes (325 degrees). Bread crumbs can be stored only for three or four days and then need to be kept in the freezer. The size of the crumbs is about the size of small peas.

Stage 4: JBmeal. This stage of bread is the most versatile and can be added to many of your favorite recipes. The bread must dry completely to create the JBmeal. This can be done either by letting it dry where the air can circulate around it (cut in large pieces and covered loosely with a towel or plastic wrap) or it can be placed on a cookie sheet in the oven at 200 degrees for an hour or until it is completely dry. There should be no moisture left in the bread. Break the bread into smaller pieces, place it in the food processor, and grind until it is a very fine meal. If you don't have a food processor, break the bread into small pieces and roll with a rolling pin between two sheets of wax paper or in a heavy plastic bag for the same results. Store the JBmeal, like flour or rice, in a tightly-covered container. A half a loaf makes about 2½ cups of JBmeal.

A word of caution: this bread is very filling. It is best not to have too many dishes made with Johnny bread at the same meal. Good as it is, moderation is the best rule.

Johnny bread is seductive but dangerous.
When fresh, it seduces with its crusty exterior
and soft interior. When a few days old, it assaults
the digestive system with its concrete qualities.
One would be well advised, then, to follow
Stoltz's recipes for stale Johnny bread.
She cares for your health.

Roger Nierengarten

Seasoned Bread Crumbs

Seasoned bread crumbs will keep longer than fresh crumbs. They can be seasoned in a variety of ways. Use the following recipe as a starter or as a way to launch your creativity.

Ingredients:
1/3 cup olive oil
1 tbsp butter
2 large or 3 medium cloves of garlic
salt and pepper
2 cups JBcrumbs

Preparation:
Heat oil and butter in frying pan. Add thick slices of fresh garlic. Let the garlic season the oil, cooking it slowly over low heat; do not let it darken. Remove garlic and add 1/2 tsp salt.

Pour in JBcrumbs, stirring to coat. Continue stirring while the crumbs toast for 3 or 4 minutes. Remove from heat and add another 1/2 tsp salt and freshly ground pepper.

Other spices may be added at this time: for example, mix together in a small bowl, 1 tsp dried oregano, 1 tsp dried thyme, 1/2 tsp cayenne pepper, 1 tsp paprika. Stir together and sprinkle over the bread crumbs. Mix thoroughly. Be creative and mix together various seasonings to suit your own taste.

Store seasoned JBcrumbs in a plastic bag or small jar in a cool place.

BREAKFAST DISHES

Good starts for productive days

The recipes in this section use JBslices (1), JBcrumbs (3), and JBmeal (4)

When thirty monks arose at three,
They donned their robes with conscious speed,
In dark so deep they could not see.
There was much dough they had to knead.

Some bowed their heads in silent prayer,
As others brought in baskets neat
And lined them up with patient care,
All filled with flour, salt, and wheat.

With jugs of water, cold and clear,
And tubs of sugar, lard, and yeast.
They brought in gluten flour—and beer
(This last for them—blessed by a priest.)

The thirty monks stood in a row
And, measuring out in proper part,
They mixed by hand the sticky dough,
Then kneaded it with skill and art.

Each loaf rose up at least an hour
And gained a shape both high and round.
They punched them down with ample power;
Each rose again into a mound.

Soon scores of loaves were lowered down
To ovens banked to store up heat.
The crusts turned crisp and golden brown,
The center soft with nubs of wheat.

By breakfast time the loaves were done,
As hungry boys began their day.
They filled their plates, each one by one,
And with one voice, they stood to say:

"This bread maintains our thinking skill,
So give us each another slice,
We'll tell you when we've had our fill:
Delicious bread—beyond a price.

"It's Johnny bread that keeps us here,
And later on tempts us to buy
More bread to eat with cheese and beer.
And now you know exactly why

"We thank the work of all those monks;
To God all glory do they give.
But we'll not get and pack our trunks;
We share their bread—that's how we live!"

Richard Nicolai

Applesauce Quick Bread   ** breakfast (4)

Delicious and especially good when made with crisp fall apples from the Collegeville Fruit Farm.

Ingredients:
1 egg
1 cup applesauce (unsweetened)
1/4 cup melted butter or margarine
1/2 cup dark brown sugar, packed
1/4 cup white sugar

1 1/2 cups flour
1/2 cup JBmeal
2 tsp baking powder
1/2 tsp baking soda
1/2 tsp salt
1 tsp ground cinnamon
1/2 tsp grated nutmeg

1/2 cup raisins
1/2 cup chopped pecans or walnuts

Preparation:
Beat together egg and applesauce, add butter and sugars; mix well. In a separate bowl measure the dry ingredients: flour, JBmeal, baking powder, soda, salt, spices; stir well. Carefully stir the dry ingredients into the egg mixture.* Add raisins and nuts, making sure the additions are fully incorporated. Spoon bread batter into a greased and floured 9-by-5-inch loaf pan.

Bake in a 350 degree oven for about an hour (until a toothpick inserted in the center comes out clean). Let stand in the pan for 10 minutes before turning out the loaf; cool on a rack or a thickness of paper towels.

*With quick breads such as this (breads not using yeast as the leavening agent), the less you stir the batter, the lighter the bread will be.

Try it toasted.

Fr. Walter
Reger, OSB

8

Banana Crumb Coffee Cake   ** breakfast (3)

This cake is good right out of the oven for breakfast, or as it cools, as a dessert cake. Versatile and delicious.

Ingredients
1/3 cup canola oil or vegetable oil
1 large egg
1/2 cup milk
1/2 tsp vanilla
1 cup sugar
2 medium, very ripe bananas, mashed
1 3/4 cups flour
2 tsp baking powder
1/4 tsp salt

Crumb topping
1/2 cup very fine bread crumbs
3 tbsp soft butter
1/4 cup brown sugar

Preparation:
Beat egg, oil, and sugar together until well creamed. Add milk, vanilla, and bananas. Mix well. Sift together flour, baking powder, and salt; add to mixture, stirring only until well combined.

Mix JBcrumbs, butter, and brown sugar for the topping together with pastry blender or with your fingers until the consistency of peas. Set aside.

Spoon batter into buttered 8-inch square baking dish. Sprinkle with crumb mixture.

Bake in 375 degree oven for 25 to 30 minutes.

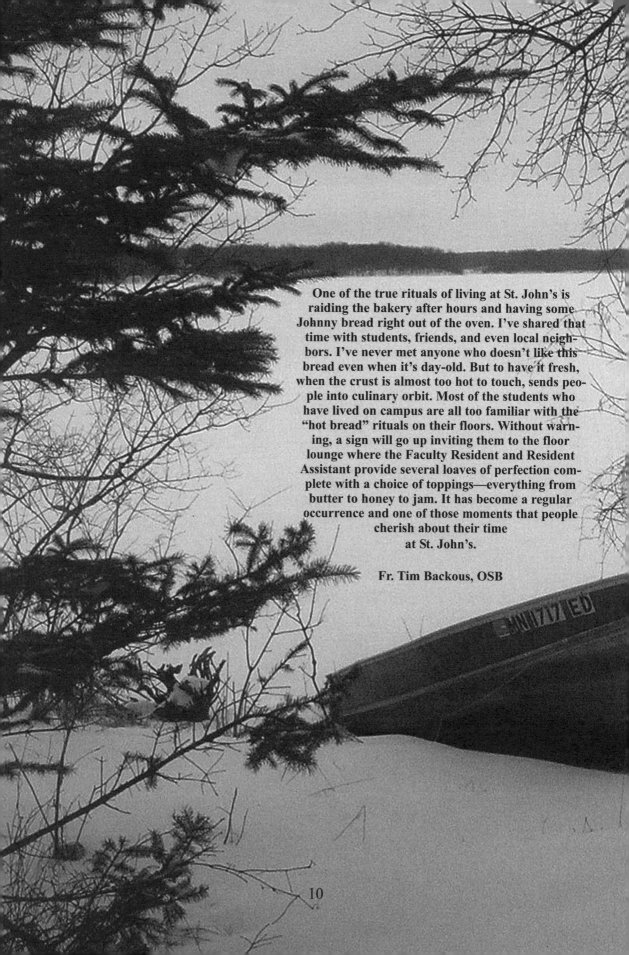

One of the true rituals of living at St. John's is raiding the bakery after hours and having some Johnny bread right out of the oven. I've shared that time with students, friends, and even local neighbors. I've never met anyone who doesn't like this bread even when it's day-old. But to have it fresh, when the crust is almost too hot to touch, sends people into culinary orbit. Most of the students who have lived on campus are all too familiar with the "hot bread" rituals on their floors. Without warning, a sign will go up inviting them to the floor lounge where the Faculty Resident and Resident Assistant provide several loaves of perfection complete with a choice of toppings—everything from butter to honey to jam. It has become a regular occurrence and one of those moments that people cherish about their time at St. John's.

Fr. Tim Backous, OSB

Granola

The gravelly goodness of Johnny bread adds extra heartiness to this breakfast standby.

Ingredients:
4 cups oatmeal
1/2 cup wheat germ or wheat bran
1 cup unsalted sunflower seeds
1 cup coconut
1/2 cup JBmeal

Add any or all of the following four ingredients:
1 tsp cinnamon
1 tsp grated lemon rind
1 cup raisins
3/4 cup slivered almonds.

1/2 cup honey
1/3 cup canola oil

Preparation:
In a large bowl mix dry ingredients together. Add desired flavorings. Melt honey until warm; pour honey and oil over dry mixture and stir until all is moistened. Spread granola onto two large, ungreased cookie sheets and bake in 300 degree oven for 30 minutes, stirring mixture every 10 minutes to toast evenly.

Cool. Store in canister. Tastes great with sliced bananas and milk, or try it with yogurt and dried cranberries.

When I wished to share pride, I brought this simple gift home. If custom desired one bring his part to the table, I carted the inelegant loaf with me. A countertop seemed bare without the familiar wrapper, the familiar history . . . such common effort baked to satiate the senses within a timeline of tradition and, in hindsight, given as a glimpse of royal abundance.

Perhaps the breaking of such bread rooted me in tempests. Conceivably, the ingredients illuminated the possibilities of common grains or maybe, when conversation required eloquence, the food allowed me to stand silent. But it is still bread: a sturdy, coarse variety refined by heritage. And I value its use.

Shaun Johnson

Oatmeal Breakfast Bread   ** breakfast (4)

The tasty JBmeal in this recipe creates a delicious quick bread.

Ingredients:
1/2 cup oatmeal (uncooked rolled oats)
1 1/4 cups buttermilk

2/3 cup JBmeal
3/4 cup flour
1 tsp ground cinnamon
1 tsp ground ginger
1 tsp baking soda
1 tsp baking powder
1/4 tsp salt
1/2 cup sugar

2 eggs
1/2 cup melted butter
1/2 cup chopped walnuts
1/2 cup golden raisins

Preparation:

Stir oatmeal into the mixing bowl with measured buttermilk. Let stand for 15 to 30 minutes or until oatmeal is thoroughly soaked.

While the oatmeal is softening, in a separate bowl stir together all the dry ingredients: JBmeal, flour, spices, baking soda, baking powder, salt, and sugar. Set aside.

Add eggs and melted butter to the buttermilk mixture and beat well. Stir in the dry ingredients with the raisins and nuts, mixing only until blended.

Pour into a greased and floured 9-by-5-inch loaf pan. Bake in 350 degree oven for 50 to 60 minutes, until a wooden toothpick inserted into the center of the loaf comes out clean. After baking, let loaf rest in pan for 10 minutes; remove from pan, and cool on a rack or a thickness of paper towels. Serve with honey walnut cream cheese or your favorite jam.

Honey Walnut Cream Cheese
4 oz cream cheese
1 tbsp honey
1/2 cup finely chopped walnuts

Let cream cheese soften to room temperature while bread bakes. Stir cream cheese in a small bowl until the consistency of soft butter. Add honey and mix well. Stir in walnuts.

Just Another Veteran's Benefit

Some of us returned from the military in 1957 to resume our study at St. John's. We had joined up to get the G.I. Bill. Our government provided us with $110.00 per month. Towards the end of most months, we Day Hop Vets had spent most of that sum paying for rent, eggs, sausage, beer, and other essentials. On those lean days, two slices from a loaf of Johnny bread kept in a locker in the hall outside the "Caf" would make a great ketchup-and-mustard sandwich with those condiments kept on every table by Joe Spanier. How much better could it get?

Larry Poston

Raisin Bran JB Muffins

A healthy way to start a morning or to keep up the energy level during the day. Nutritious and tasty.

Ingredients:
4 tbsp butter, melted
1 egg
1 cup buttermilk
juice of 1/2 lemon (about 2 or 3 tbsp)
1/3 cup dark brown sugar, packed
1/4 cup granulated sugar

2/3 cup flour
1/3 cup JBmeal
1/4 cup whole wheat flour
1/2 cup wheat bran
1 1/2 tsp baking soda
1/4 tsp salt
1 tsp cinnamon

1/2 cup raisins
1/4 cup chopped walnuts (optional)

Preparation:
In mixing bowl combine melted butter, egg, buttermilk, lemon juice, and sugars; mix well. In a separate bowl stir together all the dry ingredients: flour, JBmeal, whole wheat flour, bran, baking soda, cinnamon, and salt.

Add the dry ingredients to the milk and egg mixture. Mix only until combined. Stir in raisins. Grease or spray muffin tin; fill muffins cups 3/4 full.

Bake in a 400 degree oven for 15 to 20 minutes. Makes 12 to 15 muffins.

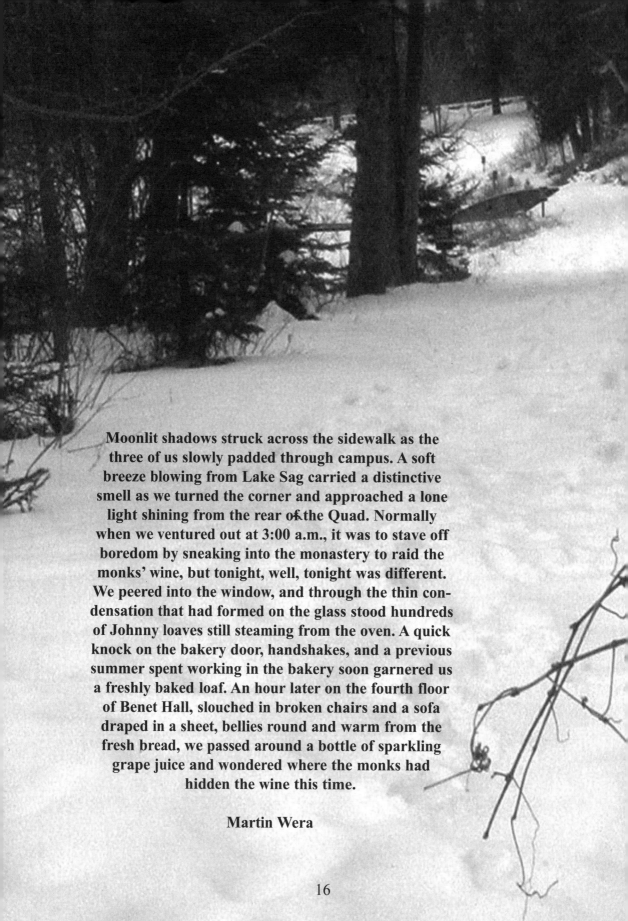

Moonlit shadows struck across the sidewalk as the three of us slowly padded through campus. A soft breeze blowing from Lake Sag carried a distinctive smell as we turned the corner and approached a lone light shining from the rear of the Quad. Normally when we ventured out at 3:00 a.m., it was to stave off boredom by sneaking into the monastery to raid the monks' wine, but tonight, well, tonight was different. We peered into the window, and through the thin condensation that had formed on the glass stood hundreds of Johnny loaves still steaming from the oven. A quick knock on the bakery door, handshakes, and a previous summer spent working in the bakery soon garnered us a freshly baked loaf. An hour later on the fourth floor of Benet Hall, slouched in broken chairs and a sofa draped in a sheet, bellies round and warm from the fresh bread, we passed around a bottle of sparkling grape juice and wondered where the monks had hidden the wine this time.

Martin Wera

Stearns County Quiche   ** breakfast (1)

This dish is one of my favorites. Mix it up the night before or stir it up and pop it in the oven before you go to church. A wonderful smell will greet hardy appetites. A good main dish for a cool fall-day brunch or for a cheerful gathering around an afternoon fire.

Ingredients
2 to 3 green onions with a good portion of the green, chopped
1 cup cheddar cheese, grated
2 cups ham, cut into cubes—not lunchmeat (or you also could
    use chicken or sausage that has been precooked)
1/2 loaf of day-old JBslices, crusts removed
1/2 cup JBcrumbs

4 cups whole milk
8 eggs

Preparation:
Butter both sides of the bread sparingly, placing one layer of bread to cover the bottom of a 9-by-13-inch pan. Sprinkle bread with half of the onion, then cheese, and then ham. Cover with another layer of bread and repeat filling.

Mix eggs and milk together. Pour over the mixture and refrigerate (2 to 24 hours). When ready to bake, sprinkle top with JBcrumbs. Bake for one hour and 15 minutes at 350 degrees. It's best served with mushroom sauce.

Mushroom sauce
2 tbsp butter
2 tbsp flour
1 cup hot milk
2 cups of sliced mushrooms sautéed in 4 tbsp butter
Salt and pepper to taste

Saute mushrooms in sizzling butter until soft. Set aside.

In a heavy-bottomed saucepan melt 2 tbsp butter. Add flour and stir over medium heat until mixture browns. Turn off the heat. Add hot milk and whisk vigorously as mixture thickens (add a bit more milk if necessary to make the sauce the consistency you desire). Stir in mushrooms.

Or add sautéed mushrooms to a can of undiluted cream of mushroom soup. Heat thoroughly. If you add a tablespoon or so of sherry to the soup, no one will know the sauce comes from a can.

St. John's bread has been a standard by which bread is judged in Stearns County for decades. One significant change has been in its formula for milling.

The country is generally slow to change: local breweries have stood against big takeovers; some have survived as Cold Spring has. The Freeport mill was slow to surrender. There were at least five notable sausage makers—at my last count—Plantenburg in Richmond, Ebnet in Albany, Knaus in Kimball, one in Holdingford, and one in Cold Spring. During Prohibition, there were at least three approved moonshines, the basic ingredient being a hybrid corn which gave its name to the liquor: Minnesota 13.

St. John's bread surrendered its original standard under pressure of stomach disorders among monks and others sometime in the '40s and '50s. Liberals in the monastery were for change; conservatives against. There had been no comparable disagreement in the community, well, except that over the homogenization of milk.

The problem was the whole grains of wheat which ignored the milling process and showed up in the bread. It was too much for the human stomach to handle. The problem was comparable to one in the animal world. Aardvarks cannot eat ants which have hard shells. Aardvarks have no gizzards, and therefore, have to survive on termites which have neither bones nor hard shells. Chickens have gizzards which grind whole wheat. The no gizzard condition of human beings determined the case in favor of changing the grinding standard for the flour. Thus the change in the bread.

Eugene J. McCarthy

MAIN COURSES

Nutritious, satisfying entrees

The recipes in this section use JBcubes (2) and JBcrumbs (3)

It is the custom to take a big box of Johnny bread to all Johnny Stand-ups around the country. Several years ago this story was reported about Fr. Roger Botz and Thom Woodward representing St. John's at a reunion in Los Angeles. Their plane was late coming to California, and as they hurried from the airport in their rented car, they puzzled over the directions to the Stand-up. The reunion, at a posh site, when they found it, was surrounded by a parking lot lined with expensive foreign cars—Jaguars, Mercedes, BMWs, among others. They quickly turned over the keys of their car to the valet, rushed inside, and joined the milling, joshing, jostling people, jockeying for a place at the bar until, aghast, Fr. Roger hoarsely whispered to Thom, "We forgot, we forgot the bread in the car." "Not to worry," said Thom, "just go to the valet and ask him to bring up the car." Fr. Roger hurried off. Finding the valet, he asked him just that; the valet responded with his own question: "Did you have the Rolls?" "No," burst out Fr. Roger. "I had the unsliced bread."

Salads with Croutons * entree (2)

Included with the instructions for making croutons are two salad recipes in which the croutons work well. Each salad could be served as complete meal.

Croutons:

Using day-old sliced bread, brush the JBslices with olive oil or melted butter. Leave plain or season the slices as desired: a bit of cayenne pepper mixed with salt, pepper, and a bit of garlic powder; or garlic salt; or a light sprinkling of grated parmesan cheese. Place on cookie sheet in 375 degree oven for 10 to 15 minutes. Remove from oven and with a sharp knife, cut into 1- or 2-inch squares. Add croutons to a salad at the very last minute to keep them from becoming soggy.

Caesar Salad

One head of romaine lettuce, washed, spun dry, or blotted dry with paper towels. Store for an hour or so in a plastic bag in the refrigerator. Tear into serving pieces. A few red onion slices mixed in with the lettuce will give it an added flavor.

Caesar Salad Dressing
1 large or 2 medium eggs, room temperature
1/8 tsp salt
freshly ground pepper
1/2 cup olive oil
4 tbsp lemon juice
1 cup freshly grated parmesan cheese
4 to 6 flat anchovies (if desired*)

Bring 3 cups salted water to a boil; carefully spoon whole, uncracked eggs into boiling water for 15 seconds. Remove and set aside. In a large salad bowl, place crisp romaine lettuce pieces. Add salt, pepper, olive oil, and gently toss (your hands work the best for this).

Then break the eggs on top of the salad, add the lemon juice, and mix again until the lettuce is thoroughly coated with the dressing. Add cheese and anchovies (if desired) and mix again. Scatter the croutons (10 or 12) on top and serve immediately. Grilled chicken breast or shrimp can also be added.

*You may use anchovy paste instead of the canned anchovies. About an inch or two of the paste out of the tube will substitute—or suit your own taste. Mix paste with the lemon juice before adding the juice to the salad.

My mother is a Minnesotan transplant, born and raised by a Johnny grad. She and her brothers would occasionally get a loaf around Homecoming time when she was a little girl. Many years and several moves down the line, she raised three boys in Iowa. In an unexplained pattern of reverse-migration, all three of us have in turn attended St. John's. For the past eight years we have had numerous caravans running between Collegeville and Cedar Rapids. The baggage we carried was usually a heap of dirty clothes, books, and music. For color we added an occasional passenger or companion as it was a fairly long trip to make alone. The one static commodity we always picked up at the last minute was a couple loaves of Johnny bread. Mom loves to cook it, toast it, eat it with honey, and she loves to give it away to our neighbors as Minnesotan "ethnic" food. Visitors to our house always knew when one of her boys was visiting home because of the pile of brown bread stacked on the fridge.

Ryan Poindexter

Salad with Croutons

Seared Beef Salad with Blue Cheese Dressing (a recipe from Ireland)
    6 to 8 ounces of lean sirloin, top round, or any tender piece of beef loin
    1 tbsp olive oil
    1/2 tsp salt
    2 tsp coarsely ground pepper

Make sure meat is trimmed and free of fat and sinew. Slice beef across the grain into thin slices (between 1/4- and 1/2-inch thick). Season with salt and pepper. Heat 1 tbsp oil in heavy frying pan until very hot and add meat, frying briefly on each side until seared. Frying it longer will make the meat tough. Divide the slices into 3 or 4 batches, frying one batch at a time so that slices will not be crowded. Add more oil to the pan if you need it. Lightly salt and pepper to taste. Set aside.

Ingredients:
    1 cup celery, sliced diagonally
    1 thinly sliced cucumber, peeled if the cucumber has been waxed
    2 or 3 green onions, sliced diagonally
    1 cup grape tomatoes or halved cherry tomatoes
    Romaine or red leaf lettuce, rinsed, dried, torn into serving pieces,
        chilled

Preparation:
Place vegetables all in a bowl together except the lettuce.

Vinaigrette
    2 tbsp vinegar—apple cider or balsamic
    1/2 tsp Dijon mustard
    1/2 tsp brown sugar
    1/4 cup olive oil
    Coarsely ground pepper
    1/4 tsp salt
    1/2 cup crumbled blue cheese

To make dressing, combine vinegar, mustard, sugar, salt, and pepper in small bowl; whisk. Continue to whisk while slowly pouring in olive oil until mixture combines. Add crumbled blue cheese. Stir.

To assemble: on large dinner plates pile crisp, cold lettuce, sprinkled with a pinch of salt. Divide and place on each plate on top of lettuce: celery, onions, tomatoes, and cucumber. Arrange slices of beef decoratively on each salad. Pour dressing over salads. Add croutons; garnish with a tablespoon of snipped chives or chopped parsley.

Serves 2 or 3.

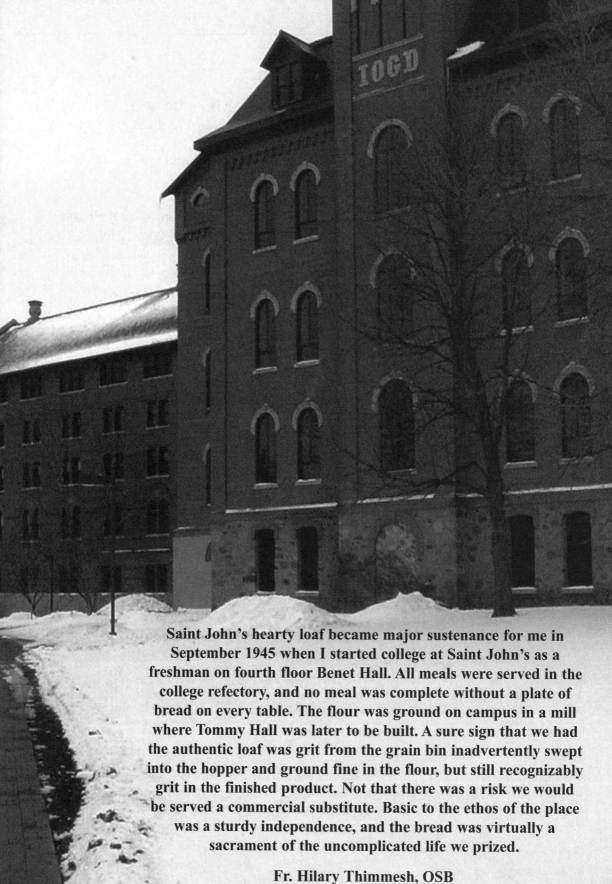

Saint John's hearty loaf became major sustenance for me in September 1945 when I started college at Saint John's as a freshman on fourth floor Benet Hall. All meals were served in the college refectory, and no meal was complete without a plate of bread on every table. The flour was ground on campus in a mill where Tommy Hall was later to be built. A sure sign that we had the authentic loaf was grit from the grain bin inadvertently swept into the hopper and ground fine in the flour, but still recognizably grit in the finished product. Not that there was a risk we would be served a commercial substitute. Basic to the ethos of the place was a sturdy independence, and the bread was virtually a sacrament of the uncomplicated life we prized.

Fr. Hilary Thimmesh, OSB

Spaghetti with Shrimp   ** entree (3)

A quick dish to put together that will stick to your ribs; tasty with a bit of a snap to it.

Ingredients
1 pound spaghetti
1 cup JBcrumbs
1 tbsp butter plus 1 tbsp olive oil
6 tbsp olive oil
3 medium garlic cloves, minced
2 to 3 tbsp lemon juice
3 tbsp minced fresh parsley
1/2 tsp dried, hot red pepper flakes or to taste
1 pound medium-sized shrimp (shelled and deveined), fresh or
frozen

Preparation
Bring 4 quarts of water to boil; salt the water and add spaghetti.

While the pasta cooks, heat 1 tbsp butter and 1 tbsp oil in frying pan. Add JBcrumbs and toast for about 5 minutes, stirring until crumbs are a bit crunchy. Set aside. Wipe out pan and return to heat.

In frying pan add 6 tbsp olive oil; when oil gets hot, add minced garlic and cook for about 5 to 10 seconds—do not let the garlic get too brown. Immediately add chopped parsley, hot pepper, and lemon juice. Lower the heat and cook for about 30 seconds. Add shrimp, stirring frequently until shrimp are heated through (if they are frozen) or if they are fresh, until they turn pink—about 3 to 5 minutes more.

Adjust the seasonings (does it need more hot, more salt, pepper? Suit the sauce to your taste). Remove from heat.

When the pasta is cooked, firm to the bite (al dente), drain it quickly, leaving it still moist; transfer it to a large bowl. Add the sauce and bread crumbs. Toss gently. Garnish with chopped parsley.

Serves 4.

Jerry Mead was former head of the dining service here in the late '60s. He was something of an entrepreneur and took over the commercial aspects of St. John's bread when Fr. Walter stepped down. Fr. Walter had worked for years trying to get a loaf on grocers' shelves that had the look and "feel" of the bread baked on campus. Commercial bakeries always added far too much water to the mix because they sensed the need for more moisture to prolong shelf life, a major "flaw" in the reproduction of the real stuff. One day Jerry Mead returned to campus after yet one more session with the commercial bakers. He carried a loaf of bread in each hand. As he met a colleague in front of the Abbey Church, he held up one of the loaves and said with a broad smile: "I think we've got it!" His colleague took the loaf, held it on his outstretched hand and noticed a "sag" at each end. "I'm afraid not, Jerry," he responded. "Too soft. With a good loaf of Johnny bread you have to be able to dent a car fender."

Lee Hanley

Baked Stuffed Fish with Lemon or Vermouth   ** entree (3)

This full-flavored dish is good served with parsley potatoes or steamed carrots and broccoli, and a plain green salad. To reduce the fat, mix the boiled potatoes with 1/2 cup yogurt combined with 3 tbsp chopped green onion and 3 tbsp chopped peeled cucumber.

Ingredients:
    8 small or 4 large fish fillets
    3 tbsp melted butter or olive oil
    Salt and pepper to taste

    3 cups JBcrumbs
    1/2 cup chopped celery
    1/2 cup chopped green onion
    1/2 cup chopped parsley
    1 tsp each of thyme, marjoram, tarragon

    2 tbsp lemon juice or vermouth
    1 egg
    1/2 cup chicken broth or vermouth

Preparation:
Coat fish fillets sparingly with melted butter or olive oil; season with salt and pepper to taste.

In a large mixing bowl, combine the 3 cups of JBcrumbs, chopped celery, green onion, parsley, thyme, marjoram, and tarragon. Mix thoroughly. Whisk egg with lemon juice or vermouth. Pour egg and lemon juice over the bread crumb mixture; stir until all is moistened.

Place half the fillets on an oiled baking dish. Spread the stuffing over them and top with the remaining fillets. Bake uncovered in a 350 degree oven for 25 to 30 minutes or until done; baste occasionally with the 1/2 cup of chicken broth. The fish will be juicy and flaky.

Serves 4 to 6.

DESSERTS

Sweet and Satisfying

The recipes in this section use JBcubes (2) and JBmeal (4)

Final approval of my daughter's
college choice came when I realized
that it meant a steady supply
of Johnny bread.
George Wacek

30

Chocolate Bread Pudding   ** dessert (2)

An elegant version of the ordinary bread pudding, this dish is lovely served with a dab of whipped cream and a few ripe raspberries.

Ingredients:
        2 one-ounce squares of unsweetened chocolate
        1 cup sugar
        1 1/3 cups milk
        1 cup day-old JBcubes, gently pulled apart into small pieces
        (cut off crusts for these cubes; the softer inside of the bread
                gives the pudding its delicacy)

        2 eggs
        1/4 tsp salt
        1/2 tsp vanilla

Preparation:
Over slow heat in a heavy-bottomed pan or in a double boiler, melt chocolate with sugar and 2/3 cup milk (half of the milk). Add butter and stir until melted. Set aside.

In a bowl beat eggs until light; add salt, vanilla, and the remaining 2/3 cup milk. Slowly pour a small stream of the hot chocolate mixture into the eggs, steadily stirring, heating the mixture very slowly so that the eggs won't separate and begin cooking. When the egg mixture is warmed, pour it back into the pan with the remaining chocolate mixture. Add JBcubes and stir. Return to heat and cook slowly until thick.

Pour into buttered two-quart casserole dish and bake at 350 degrees for about 30 minutes. Serve soon out of the oven. This is like a souffle—it will sink as it cools.

Serves 4.

Chocolate Chip Etc. Cookies ** dessert (4)

A variation of the favorite cookie, this one boasts an old world sturdiness provided by the JBmeal along with the oatmeal, nuts, coconut, and raisins. Good to eat and good for you!

Ingredients:
1 cup butter or margarine at room temperature
2/3 cup white sugar
2/3 cup packed brown sugar
2 eggs
1 tsp vanilla

2 cups flour
1/2 tsp baking soda
1/2 tsp salt

1/2 cup JBmeal
1/2 cup oatmeal
1 to 2 cups chocolate chips
1 cup grated coconut
1/2 cup walnuts, coarsely chopped
1/2 cup golden or regular raisins

Preparation:
Cream butter and sugars until smooth; add eggs and beat until well blended. Add vanilla.

Sift flour with soda and salt, and add to mixture. Stir in JBmeal, oatmeal, chocolate chips, coconut, nuts, and raisins. Drop by spoonful onto greased cookie sheet 1 1/2 inches apart. Bake for 12 minutes until golden brown in 375 degree oven. Cool on wire rack or paper towels, and store in airtight container.

Makes about 4 dozen cookies.

Paul Doerner was one of those World War II veterans who returned to be a Johnny after the war. He loved St. John's, never missed a football game, never tired of imitating the old monks, singing Hank William songs, drinking beer, or telling jokes. He was a man of strong opinions and later, as a judge, a firm enforcer of justice, never missing an opportunity to teach from the Bench. He married late in life, and after ten years of marriage, he and his wife were in a bad car accident. Dorothea died, and Paul became a lonely bachelor again. He developed stomach cancer the following month and wasn't eating much. One day, I called to ask if he'd like me to fix something. He said, "Maybe a little Johnny bread with honey, and tea." He laughed that afternoon and told stories about Dorothea. Paul died a week later on his wife's birthday.

EAS

Honors Chocolate Chip Cookies   ** dessert (4)

This chocolate chip cookie recipe raises the genre to high elegance. And Johnny bread adds a distinctive taste to the fine blend of flavors. Absolutely delicious cookies.

Ingredients:
1 cup butter or half shortening/half butter
3/4 cup sugar
3/4 cup packed brown sugar
2 large eggs
1 tsp vanilla

2 cups flour
1 1/2 cup oatmeal, blended in food processor until finely
   ground
1 cup JBmeal
1/2 tsp salt
1 tsp baking soda
1 tsp baking powder

3 (1.5 oz) milk chocolate bars, grated
1 cup chocolate chips
1 cup chopped pecans or walnuts

Preparation:
Cream sugars and butter together until smooth; add 2 eggs plus the vanilla and beat well.

Sift together flour, salt, soda, and baking powder; add to this mixture the blended oatmeal and JBmeal. Stir together. Slowly incorporate dry ingredients into the egg mixture.

Mix grated chocolate, chocolate chips, and nuts into the cookie dough until distributed throughout. Dough will be stiff.

Roll into 2-inch balls and place 1 1/2 inches apart on a greased cookie sheet. Flatten cookies slightly. Bake in a 375 degree oven for 10 to 12 minutes. Do not overbake.

Remove from oven and cool on a rack; store in airtight container.

Makes about 5 dozen irresistible cookies.

"I'm perplexed," the young student said,
When buying renowned Johnny bread,
"Why those bread-maker Monks
Bake gigantic bread hunks;
It taxes the brains in my head."

Jim Rickman

JB Cheesecake *** dessert (4)

This cheesecake has been a family favorite for many, many years. The recipe comes from a good friend, Jim Backas, who as a chef at a resort in northern Michigan, adapted it to suit his taste. The Johnny bread enhances its texture, setting off the creaminess of the filling.

Crust:
- 3/4 cup crushed graham crumbs
- 3/4 cup JB meal
- 1/4 cup sugar
- 1/2 cup melted butter

Mix all ingredients together. (Reserve 2 tbsp for topping to use after the cake has baked.) Press mixture firmly into the bottom of spring form mold or a 10-inch pie plate, extending the crust to an inch or so up the sides of the mold. It works best to press mixture with the flat bottom of a cup or measuring cup.

Filling:
- 13 ounces cream cheese (Do not use no-fat!)
- 3/4 cup sour cream (Do not use no-fat!)
- 5 eggs
- 1/2 cup sugar
- 1 tsp vanilla

Make sure the cream cheese is at room temperature; whip until smooth and creamy. Add sour cream and whip again on high until thoroughly combined and the texture again is smooth and creamy. Mix in sugar and vanilla; then add the eggs, one at a time, just until incorporated, scraping down the sides of the bowl and the beater(s) after each addition.

Pour batter into crust and smooth the top. Place on a cookie sheet in the oven. Bake in 325 degree oven until the center just barely jiggles when the pan is tapped, 45 to 50 minutes. Do not overbake.

Make a topping of sour cream or yogurt (about 3/4 cup) with sugar and vanilla to taste (about 3 to 4 tbsp sugar to 1 tsp vanilla and a pinch of salt). Spread over entire top of cheesecake while it is still very warm. Sprinkle with the reserved crust mixture. Chill for several hours in the refrigerator. (In a Minnesota winter, the porch will do.)

My mother or the hired girl (my kids can't get over the term!) baked bread at least three times a week, wonderful bread—raisin bread, cinnamon bread, rye bread, white and whole wheat bread. I remember coming home from school in the late spring and having warm bread with spring onions, fresh peas and ham cooked together in light cream. Then at St. John's I couldn't get used to that denser, heavier Johnny bread.

I remember my mother saying when we didn't finish something on our plate to "remember the poor starving Chinese." At SJU my freshman year, seated at a table with a monk to keep us halfway civilized, Peter Chou from Formosa took an uncut loaf and hit Johnny Kaiser over the head with it. I remembered my mother's words, but on the other hand, I thought it a perfect use for the too-heavy bread.

Robert Shafer

JB Raspberry Torte with Bittersweet Chocolate Ganache   *** dessert (4)

This dessert, adapted from Gourmet *magazine, imparts an elegant touch to the familiar Johnny bread flavor. The texture of the bread gives the torte its nut-like quality.*

Ingredients:
1 1/2 cups JBmeal
3 tbsp flour
1/4 tsp salt
4 large eggs, room temperature
2/3 cup light brown sugar, packed
1 tsp vanilla
1/4 cup melted and slightly cooled butter
1/2 cup heavy whipping cream
7 ounces bittersweet chocolate, chopped
good raspberry jam (about a cup)

Procedure:
Butter a jelly roll pan or cookie sheet, 15x10x1 inches. Line the pan with waxed paper or parchment cooking paper. Butter the paper; sprinkle with flour, shaking pan so that just enough flour adheres to the butter; discard rest. Set aside.

Combine JBmeal, flour, salt in a bowl. Stir to combine.

In a mixer beat together eggs, brown sugar, and vanilla on high for about five minutes until mixture triples in volume—eggs will become pale yellow and foamy. (To beat by hand, this will take probably 10 minutes or so.) Gently fold crumb mixture into the eggs, adding about a fourth of the mixture at a time. To the cooled, melted butter (in a separate bowl) add about a cup of the batter and combine. Now carefully fold the butter mixture back into the batter.

Pour batter onto buttered, lined cookie sheet and gently tap bottom of pan on surface to let the air bubbles break. Place cookie sheet in the middle of a 350 degree oven for 10 to 14 minutes. (Check after 10 min). Remove from oven when edges are lightly browned and top looks dry. Let stand in pan for 10 minutes. Then gently invert torte onto cutting surface; remove paper and thoroughly cool before cutting.

Ganache *(French word for dark chocolate combined with heavy cream, cooked to a luscious thickness)*
Mix together in a heavy-bottomed saucepan over low heat, the chocolate and whipping cream. Stir until mixture is smooth and melted. Do not let it boil or chocolate will turn to curds. Chill ganache in refrigerator or over cold water until it thickens, stirring occasionally. This should take half an hour or so.

To assemble the torte:
Slice torte into 5 equal strips across the width of the cake, approximately 10 inches by 3 inches each. Take one of the strips and place it on a plate or platter. Spread the top with raspberry jam. Add another strip on top of this one, spread it with jam; continue until all the layers have been added, leaving the top layer bare. Carefully trim sides and ends with a sharp knife so they are even. With a spatula, spread top and sides of torte with the ganache. Chill until chocolate hardens—for half an hour or so. Slice to serve. Garnish with a few raspberries, a sprig of mint, and a good dollop of whipped cream. Serves 6 to 8. Very rich.

MMMMMMMMMMMMM . . . Johnny Bread!

I am a big fan of the stuff. I am a simple man;
therefore, I try my best to avoid the complications of life,
and this is reflected in my eating habits. I am a big fan
of bread and butter. Moreover, after years of research
(almost two), I have come to the conclusion that Johnny
bread is the absolute best for simply slapping a little
butter on and goin' to town, satisfying that never-ending
hunger that I experience. Not to say that this is the
only way that I enjoy Johnny bread: I love a tasty turkey
sandwich or a good old-fashioned PB&J, and I really
go for dipping it in soup; actually I have not yet had
a Johnny bread experience that I did not enjoy. I guess
there's just a certain little something about the stuff
that just rubs me the right way. Overall, I would say
that I am a big fan of eating. I am like one of those
birds or bugs that tries to eat its own body
weight in food every day.
You can't go wrong because food is splendid.
And Johnny bread is splendid food.

Andrew Sjodin

40

College Fare

The following are easy-to-make recipes suited for the pressure of time and study for college students or people on the go. They'll give a good nutritious boost for added energy—especially when papers are due or tests are imminent.

Toad in the Hole   * college fare (1)

    a thick slice of day-old Johnny bread
    one egg

Cut a hole about the size of an egg out of the center of the bread. In a moderately hot frying pan, add 1 tbsp butter and 1 tsp of oil. (If more conscious of cutting back on fat, switch the proportions of oil to butter—the oil keeps the butter from burning, but the butter gives the bread a beautiful color as well as taste.) Add the bread to the sizzling butter, fry for 15 to 30 seconds; turn toasted bread over, add a bit more butter to the hole, if desired, and break the egg into the hole. Cook about half a minute, depending on how thoroughly cooked the yolk will be; flip over the bread and egg, just long enough to cook the egg white on top. Season with salt and pepper. Serve with fruit on the side: for example, a can of mandarin oranges with a sliced banana, garnished with slices of kiwi will give a balanced, yet colorful meal.

French Toast with Blueberry Syrup   * college fare (1)

    6 slices of 1-inch-thick day-old Johnny bread
    2 eggs
    1/2 cup milk
    1/4 tsp salt
    1 tbsp vegetable oil mixed 2 tsp butter

For the French toast: In frying pan over moderate heat, melt butter with oil. In a shallow bowl beat eggs, milk, and salt with a fork until combined. Dip pieces of bread into the mixture and fry on both sides. Serve with blueberry syrup.

Blueberry Syrup

    1 to 2 cups blueberries, frozen or fresh
    3/4 cup sugar
    1/2 cup water

In a saucepan bring blueberries, sugar, and water to a boil and simmer while the toast is cooking. (More sugar will make the syrup thicker.) Pour liberally over toast.

During a not-too-distant Christmas break, I returned to an empty home with a couple of weeks worth of laundry, a few video tapes, and a hearty loaf of Johnny bread. My younger brother was the first to arrive home, and instead of his buckling down to do his homework, we decided to pop in a movie and talk the meaningless banter at which brothers excel. After searching the house for the typical movie fare and coming up empty, we soon decided that the Johnny bread could more than adequately fill the role. Without any obstacles to breaking rules of proper etiquette, we snatched a tub of butter from the fridge and found our familiar spots in front of the TV. Reveling in our impending gluttony, we proceeded to rip hunks of bread, dip them into the butter, and pop them into our grinning mouths. Since that cold and lonely December day, we have continued this practice a couple times, and have even termed our movie snack "Benedictine Popcorn."

Bryan Bohlman

Here are a few more easy-to-make recipes that should satisfy between-classes hunger.

Kitchen Counter Pizza   * college fare (1, 3)
On a slice of Johnny bread, stack in the following order:
 1 slice of ham or several slices of pepperoni to cover the bread
 2 or 3 slices of fresh tomato
 2 rings of green pepper
 sliced onion, if desired
 1 tsp dried oregano
 freshly ground black pepper
 hot pepper flakes, if desired
 grated or thinly sliced mozzarella cheese

Place bread with all ingredients piled on top, on a square of tin foil; bake in 400 degree oven or toaster oven for about 10 to 12 minutes until all ingredients are heated through and cheese is melted. Watch so cheese doesn't burn.

Seasoned Chicken Legs
 6 chicken legs
 1/2 cup flour
 1 egg, slightly beaten with 1 tbsp milk or water
 1 cup seasoned JBcrumbs

Pour flour on a paper towel, place egg mixture in shallow bowl, and put JBcrumbs on another paper towel. Rinse and dry chicken. Roll each piece of chicken in flour, dip in egg, and then coat with seasoned breadcrumbs. Lay chicken on cookie sheet and bake in 350 degree oven for 45 to 50 minutes. Tasty and crunchy. Leftovers keep well in the fridge.

Celery and Blue Cheese
 3 to 4 sticks of celery, washed and dried
 4 ounces of blue cheese or creamed cheese or one of your favorite soft cheeses
 1/4 cup seasoned breadcrumbs

Stuff hollow of celery with cheese and dip in JBcrumbs. A hearty snack or appetizer.

Other Uses for Seasoned Breadcrumbs
Add 1/2 cup JBcrumbs to meatloaf
Sprinkle 1/3 cup over savory salads
Use as a crunchy topping for omelettes, potatoes (mashed, baked or scalloped), or other vegetables.
Bread fish or chops before frying, and then use your imagination.

I think of St. John's bread as the bread of life. And I come by that appreciation quite naturally. For years my mother baked bread every day for our family. If she couldn't do it, my father took over. Once, when Mother was sick in bed for a few days, Dad spent his mornings in the kitchen, baking bread rather than buying anemic store loaves. So when I was at St. John's, I relished Johnny bread—the crisp crust, the nutty flavor, the crunch of wheat, the yeasty aroma— especially when it came still hot from the ovens. It was, I think, the truest form of communion bread at SJU. Now, as I bake bread— always Johnny-style—I say Amen, Amen to that memory and legacy.

Richard Nicolai

Johnny-Power Bars

These bars give you the kind of lineman get-up-and-go that drives the victories for the Johnny football team.

Ingredients:
1/2 cup toasted, chopped pecans

1 1/2 cup old-fashioned oatmeal
1/2 cup JBmeal
1/2 cup raisins
1 rounded tsp cinnamon
1/4 tsp salt

3 tbsp butter
1/3 cup canola or other vegetable oil
1/3 cup packed dark brown sugar
3 tbsp honey
2 tbsp grated orange rind
1 tbsp grated lemon rind
1 tbsp lemon juice

Preparation:
Toast pecans in moderately heated frying pan for about 5 minutes until aromatic, stirring to toast evenly. Set aside to cool.

In a large bowl, mix oats, JBmeal, raisins, pecans, cinnamon, salt.

In a saucepan, combine sugar, honey, butter, and oil and heat to the boiling point, stirring to keep the mixture smooth. Pour this over the dry ingredients in bowl and mix. Add orange and lemon rind. Mix. Taste for sweetness and add a bit of lemon juice if too sweet. In buttered 8-inch square pan, pack mixture with your hand or bottom of measuring cup. Bake in 350 degree oven for about 30 minutes until golden brown on top.

It is important to cool bars in pan before proceeding with next step (or you may end up with granola!). Carefully invert pan on work surface. Cut into bars with a sharp knife. Makes about a dozen and a half bars.

This recipe can be varied to suit your taste: instead of pecans and raisins, add any combination of chopped dates, apricots, raisins, walnuts and/or dried apples. You may want to try different flavorings also. For example, omit citrus rind and add nutmeg or a teaspoon of vanilla.

BEST DINER - 2002
Hamlin's Coffee Shop
512 Nicollet Avenue
Minneapolis
(an ad from *City Pages*)

Whether you sit in one of the comfy black
leather booths or at an old-school counter,
the place retains a relaxed charm. We defy
you to find anything bad on the menu here—
or to drink more than two-thirds of your cup
of coffee before it's refilled to the brim.
Hamlin's does all the diner staples
extraordinarily well. . . . . The turkey melt,
smothered in Muenster cheese and bacon,
served on golden slices of St. John's bread,
is diner grub elevated to an art form.

Peanut Butter Johnny Bars   * college fare (4)

A sweet and satisfying snack that will carry you through to the next meal.

Ingredients:
1 1/2 cups oatmeal
1/2 cup JBmeal
1/4 cup dark brown sugar, packed

1/4 cup of canola or vegetable oil
1 tbsp butter
3 tbsp honey
3 tbsp peanut butter
1 cup miniature marshmallows.

1 tsp vanilla
1/2 cup chopped salted peanuts

Preparation:
Mix together oatmeal, JBmeal, and brown sugar in a large bowl.

In a saucepan add oil, butter, honey, peanut butter, and marshmallows. Stir over medium heat until mixture boils. Remove from heat and keep stirring until everything is melted. Add vanilla and nuts.

Pour hot mixture into dry ingredients; stir until thoroughly combined.

Spoon mixture into 9-inch square baking pan which has been lined with lightly oiled aluminum foil. Pack batter into pan, tapping it down with the bottom of a measuring cup or your hand. Bake in a 325 degree oven for 20 to 25 minutes until top is golden brown.

Remove from oven and let cool in pan. Turn pan upside down on cutting board; remove foil and slice with a sharp knife into bars. Bars will keep in cookie jar for a week or so.

Makes about a dozen bars.

Brush-bristled cornstalks stood along Highway 15 as I made my way back home for Thanksgiving. Almost three months had passed since starting at St. John's University, and here I was on the road back home. I was, supposedly, becoming a man—a process that had so far involved learning how not to destroy my clothes in the laundry and committing to memory the Refectory's weekly menu, but precious little, it seemed, about the burgeoning world around me. So, rattling across the plains amid pick-up trucks held together with rust and stubbornness, I thought hard about how I could demonstrate to my parents my hypothetical maturation into a responsible adult. Soon the wheels hit the familiar crunch of gravel and within a few minutes I stood in the front hall. After hugs and an awkward silence, I said, "So, I bought you guys a loaf of Johnny bread" in the most adult-like voice I could muster.

Martin Wera

BREADS
IN VARIOUS FORMS

Different ways to extend the taste of Johnny bread

The recipes in this section use JBslices (1) and JBmeal (4)

Dear Friend:
  Everyone who has ever been at St. John's Abbey has talked about
<u>St. John's bread</u>.
  Now selected bakers are making it and food markets are selling it.
  We invite you to join the thousands who have known this unusual
bread and are now asking for it and enjoying it.

Sincerely,
Fr. Walter Reger, OSB
1956

Bruschetta * bread (1)

Bruschetta is a heartier and larger variation of the Italian "crostini." It features large slices of bread, grilled, and often sprinkled with olive oil and rubbed with garlic. To satisfy a supper appetite, one or more of the following toppings can be added.

To prepare bruschetta: Butter or brush lightly with olive oil both sides of bread. Grill (in the oven or on the grill) till lightly brown and serve with any of the following toppings:

Fresh Tomato and Basil

  4 medium-sized Roma tomatoes, finely chopped
  1/2 cup diced celery
  2 tbsp minced parsley
  2 tbsp minced fresh sweet basil
  2 tsp white wine vinegar
  About 1/3 to 1/2 cup (to taste) extra virgin olive oil. Salt and pepper

In a bowl mix tomatoes, celery, parsley, sweet basil. Add vinegar and oil and stir until well blended. Season to taste. Top bruschetta with mixture.

The following three toppings are served warm or hot on the bruschetta. A slice of chicken breast, sliced roast beef, or even a hamburger can be an added accompaniment.

Tomato, Sage, and Red Onion

  1 tbsp olive oil
  2 tomatoes, chopped
  1 tbsp chopped sage leaves or 1 tsp ground sage
  1 red onion, thinly sliced

In a frying pan, heat olive oil. Add sliced red onion and cook briefly until onion begins to soften; add tomatoes and sage, stirring only until mixture is heated through and thoroughly combined. Season with freshly ground pepper to taste. Serve on bruschetta.

Mushroom and Peppers

  2 tbsp oil
  8 oz small, white mushrooms, sliced
  1/2 red sweet pepper, chopped
  1/2 yellow or green pepper, chopped
  1 tbsp fresh sweet basil, chopped

Heat oil in skillet; add sliced mushrooms, green and red sweet peppers, basil. Saute for 3 or 4 minutes. Add freshly ground pepper to taste, then serve on top of bruschetta.

Zucchini and Feta

  1 tbsp olive oil
  2 small zucchini, thinly sliced
  1/4 cup sundried tomatoes, in oil, chopped
  1/2 cup of feta, chopped or crumbled

Saute all ingredients until heated through and cheese is melted. Serve on bruschetta.

In Prep School in the 1950s, we ate in a big dining hall and had Johnny bread for every meal. Yes, every meal. When the bread was fresh, we young boys would eat half a dozen pieces at a sitting if we could. Fresh bread happened once a week, or maybe once every two weeks. As I think now, this probably happened on a feast day or because of something special, but we weren't paying attention. We were enjoying delicious manna. Feast day, by the way, didn't mean a day of overflowing, grand meals; it meant a saint's day or an event of similar religious importance, and it would be celebrated with a treat, like fresh bread, but certainly not with intemperance. On those days of fresh servings, for whatever reason, the bread was so good it made your taste buds squirt. We ate ravenously.

Most days, however, the bread was not served fresh. I think this was done deliberately so that we would get a more balanced diet. We used the bread then to mop up gravy or make a baloney sandwich or something like that. The baloney—made in the monastery kitchen, I suppose—was so greasy and without flavor that the bread served as an absorbent for the oozing, oily slime and neutralized the bland filling. In those days, Johnny bread was utilitarian. It kept us from starving. This was a sit-down meal, you see, and we ate what was presented or nothing.

When the meal was over, we sat quietly, waiting for everyone to finish, and then Father would say the prayers, and we could leave. This was a boring time-waster for restless fourteen-year olds. Kowalkowski, sitting across from me, decided to entertain himself one day. He placed a piece of hardened bread on a spoon, pulled it back, and fired straight at me. This was the same Kowalkowski who scored many points on the basketball court in later years and pitched for the baseball team. His aim was good. He hit me dead center in the forehead. I was taken aback by this unprovoked assault and had an immediate impulse to respond. I grabbed a spoon, scooped some soft butter, and fired back. If that shot foretold my sporting talents, I was an outfielder. The butter flew the length of the room and landed on the back slope of the head of Oogie

(continued on page 54)

In Italian this word means "little crusts." Cut out rounds of day-old Johnny bread or use thin slices with the crusts removed. These small pieces of bread are used as the base for several kinds of toppings and are generally served as appetizers.

Butter or brush lightly with olive oil both sides of the crostini. Then lightly brown on the grill or broil in oven both sides of the crostini. Arrange toppings so guests can serve themselves, or prepare the crostini in advance. Serve with the following toppings:

Olive Oil and Garlic
  1/2 cup olive oil
  3 cloves of garlic, minced
  1 tsp salt

Grill 8 to 10 slices of bread without the oil or butter. In frying pan add garlic to the heated oil. It is important not to let the garlic cook too long. 15 to 30 seconds is usually long enough, just until it is lightly browned. Dip one side of the prepared crostini into the garlic and oil, coating it generously. Keep in warm oven until serving time.

Roasted Pear and Gorgonzola Butter
  3 oz blue cheese (Gorgonzola, Roquefort, Blue)
  3 oz cream cheese
  1/4 cup butter
  1/4 cup finely chopped walnuts (optional)
  1 Bartlett or Anjou pear
  14 to 16 slices of crostini, lightly oiled and grilled

Bring cheeses and butter to room temperature. In a bowl mash cheeses and butter with a fork and stir until smooth; add chopped walnuts. Grill crostini or broil in oven. Spread each bread slice with about 1 tsp of cheese mixture and top with a slice of pear. Arrange on cookie sheet and broil again until pears are lightly browned. Serve with a sprig of mint or a sprinkle of chopped walnuts.

Black Olive and Melted Mozzarella
  1/2 cup of black olives, pitted and drained
  2 tbsp capers, drained and rinsed
  1 1/2 tsp Dijon mustard
  3 canned anchovies or 1 inch of anchovy paste from tube
  1/4 tsp dried thyme
  1 large clove garlic
  1 tbsp olive oil or canola oil
  4 ounces mozzarella cheese, thinly sliced.
  14 to 16 slices of crostini, lightly oiled and grilled

Combine all ingredients except bread and cheese in food processor. Puree. Cover each piece of grilled bread with 1 tbsp of mixture and top with a slice of mozzarella. Return to oven and broil until cheese melts, 4 to 6 minutes. Serve garnished with fresh parsley.

Enck, the biggest senior in school. His real name was Paul, but if you imagine an oogie, you know what he looked like.

He played in the middle of the line on the football team and may have been offside occasionally when his stomach hung over the line of scrimmage. He wasn't without style, however, and wore his hair greased back in a slick pompadour wave. The butter, landing softly, drew his attention, and he reached back to feel what happened, patted around, puzzled, and then rubbed around as though he were unable to tell the foreign matter from the gel that belonged there. Looking at the goo in his hand, he passed from perplexed to disgruntled. Perhaps he thought a pigeon got him, but eventually, he realized it was not hair gel; he was displeased, pissed off, you might say.

I quaked. Oogie would inquire around, I was sure, and soon learn that I had launched the gooey pigeon splat on the back of his head. I could not leave the room and hide; prayers had not been said.

Oogie turned to the row behind him and demanded, "Who did that?" George Lehner, an underclassman, farm boy, guileless, and truthful like any Catholic boy at the time, said "I did." So Oogie hit him. Strangely, George didn't seem to resent it; he seemed to think he deserved it. George, I later learned, had only moments earlier, after a fulsome meal, relaxed just a shade beyond control and released an unexpected spurt of flatulence. For this carelessness, he felt he should be hit. I was amazed at my good luck. I wasn't at ease, though. I worried that Oogie would eventually learn the full story and pay me back. It took me a few days to settle down, but nothing further came of it.

Oogie had his restitution. George felt he was treated fairly. I suffered psychic turmoil. Kowalkowski, of course, started it all with that hunk of Johnny bread and still deserves to be punished.

Don Hall

Chocolate Orange Biscotti with Almonds   ** bread (4)

This delicious twice-baked Italian cookie complements a good cup of tea. The orange and almond blend wonderfully with that familiar "gravel" taste of Johnny bread.

Ingredients:
1 cup butter (or half butter and half margarine)
2 3/4 cups sugar
4 eggs
1 tsp almond extract

4 cups sifted flour
1 cup JBmeal
2 tsp baking soda
1 tsp salt

1 1/2 cups slivered almonds
2 tbsp grated orange rind

2 good quality bittersweet chocolate bars (Lindt, for example)

Preparation:
Gently cream butter and sugar; add eggs one at a time and beat at medium speed until well blended. Add almond extract and combine thoroughly.

Sift 2 cups of the flour with the soda and salt. On low speed add sifted ingredients to the egg mixture; beat in nuts and orange rind. Add rest of flour, JBmeal, and combine. Turn mixture onto lightly floured surface and knead until mixture holds shape. (You may need a bit more flour but keep dough sticky.) Divide dough into four pieces. Shape each piece into a loaf about 12 inches long, 4 inches wide, and an inch high. Place loaves on greased cookie sheets, 2 or 3 inches apart. Bake in the middle of 325-degree oven for one hour.

Remove from oven and let cool for about 5 minutes. Place loaves on cutting board and slice diagonally into slices one-inch thick. Lay slices on cookie sheets and bake again for about 35 to 40 minutes, turning slices over after 15 minutes. Transfer to racks and cool completely.

Melt chocolate in double boiler. Frost slices with melted bittersweet chocolate or dip half of cookie in melted chocolate. Let chocolate harden before storing. Store biscotti in an airtight container at room temperature or in the fridge. Makes a lot!

Our Holy Father Benedict was so wise. He knew that we human beings could not strive to seek God without having our physical needs met. Johnny bread is part of the 1,500-year tradition of prayer, study, work, and rest that Benedict prescribed for us in his rule for beginners. Good for Benedict, good for us, good for God—I'm sure He'd like Johnny bread, too.

Eileen Derry Wallace

Italian Almond Biscotti ** bread (4)

This biscotti combines a good crunch of almonds and a wonderful orange coloring from the saffron. If you like the taste of almond, add the flavoring along with the saffron. A substantial afternoon pick-me-up.

Ingredients:
1 cup of whole, unblanched almonds

1 cup flour
1/3 cup of JBmeal
1/2 cup sugar
pinch of salt
1/8 tsp of saffron or 1/2 tsp of almond flavoring
1/2 tsp baking soda

2 eggs

Glaze: 1 egg white mixed with 1 tbsp water

Preparation:
Spread the almonds on a cookie sheet and toast in 375 degree oven for about 15 minutes. Cool. Coarsely chop 3/4 cup of the almonds. The rest of the almonds grind finely in a food processor, grinder or blender. In a bowl combine the flour, JBmeal, sugar, salt, baking soda, saffron, and ground almonds. Mix. If you are using the almond flavoring, add that to the two slightly beaten eggs. Mix the eggs into the dry ingredients, adding a bit of flour to keep the dough from being too gooey. Knead, adding the chopped almonds, until ingredients are well incorporated. Divide the dough into two parts and shape into two long logs, approximately 9-by-3 inches and about an inch high. Brush each loaf with lightly beaten egg white. Bake in a 375-degree oven on a greased and floured cookie sheet for 20 minutes.

Remove from oven and carefully place on cutting board. With a sharp knife, cut diagonally 1/2 inch slices. Lay slices on cookie sheet and return to oven set at 275 degrees. Bake again for 25 to 30 minutes more. Cool. The biscotti will be very dry and crunchy. Store in cookie jar or closely-fitted tin.

An Ode to Stale Johnny Bread

Midsummer of the year fifty-five
At St. John's I arrived, my faith to revive.
Brick buildings, green pines, twin towers surround me
Dictated my life, four seasons consecutively.
But a vision keeps its focus and shape in my head;
That delicious, hard crusted, ill-shaped Johnny bread.
Eat it while it's fresh, or you'll lose your teeth.
One day it's stale, either winter or summer heat.
Brought three loaves to my friend in California.
He accepted them politely, then fed them in absentia
to the lower animal chain, like white stones in thundering
rain. The Johnny bread remained and remained and
remained.

Cyril Paul

Symposium Bread Sticks   ** bread (4)

As good as any bread sticks you can buy, these tasty morsels are quick and easy to stir up and can be fresh out of the oven by the time dinner is on the table. My students always made these for our Christmas dinner party. A good group activity.

Ingredients:
2 1/2 cups all-purpose flour
1/2 cup JBmeal
1 tsp salt
1 tbsp sugar
1 pkg dry yeast
1/4 cup olive oil or vegetable oil
1 1/4 cup very warm water

Egg Wash
1 egg white lightly whisked with 1 tbsp water
coarse salt

Preparation:
Measure 1 cup flour, JBmeal, salt, sugar, and yeast into mixing bowl. Add oil and gradually stir in water. Beat at medium speed for 2 minutes. Add 1/2 cup more flour and beat at high speed for 2 more minutes. With a wooden spoon or on slow speed, add enough flour to make a soft dough. Knead dough, working it into a round ball. Cut into 20 equal-sized pieces. Roll each piece into a pencil shape about a foot long. Arrange an inch or so apart on an oiled cookie sheet. Paint each stick with egg wash. Sprinkle with coarse salt. Let rise in a warm spot for 10 or 15 minutes. Bake in 325 degree oven for 25 to 30 minutes.

Preparation time: 10 minutes
To Rise: 10 to 15 minutes
To Bake: 25 to 30 minutes

Johnny bread was a staple of our diet
when I was a student at St. John's in the
1950s, but it had many other uses as well,
including some that were non-nutritional.
One of my classmates, the late Len Kohler,
was a catcher on the Johnny baseball team
that I pitched for, and during practice on
one chilly spring day, he was catching me.
I was throwing as hard as I could, which
was pretty hard (later I had the
opportunity to throw those hard balls
when I played professional baseball in the
Cleveland Indians farm system). He
complained that I was hurting his hand.
It was cold and his mitt was rather worn
and he didn't have a sponge, so I sent one
of the trainers to get a couple of slices of
Johnny bread: he inserted the slices in his
mitt. It worked perfectly, and the ball
made a nice "thunk" when he caught it.
The bread was compressed but still intact
when he took it out. I'm sure it would
have made nice toast, albeit with a salty
taste of sweat and leather.

Al Eisele

Whole Wheat Come-Again Johnny Bread   *** bread (4)

A regular whole wheat bread recipe but with the added touch of "gravel" makes it a tasty poor cousin of the more hearty Johnny bread. A good way, however, to stretch the good taste. A delicious, moist bread.

Ingredients:
1 1/4 cup warm water
1 tbsp vegetable oil
2 tbsp honey
1/2 tsp salt

1 1/4 cup whole wheat flour
1 cup bread flour
1/2 cup JBmeal
1/4 cup gluten
1 1/2 tsp active dry yeast

Preparation:

Pour measured water into mixer. Add oil, honey, and salt. Mix.

In separate bowl or on paper towel, mix together all the dry ingredients and add gradually to the liquid. Beat together in mixer with bread hook for 8 to 10 minutes or knead dough until elastic, keeping dough as sticky as possible.

Place in a greased bowl, cover with kitchen towel, and set in warm place to rise until double in bulk. Punch down. Let rise again for about another hour. Punch down; let rest for 10 minutes then shape into loaf and let rise in greased loaf pan until doubled, about 45 minutes.

Bake for 30 to 35 minutes in 375-degree oven or until loaf sounds hollow when tapped. Delicious with honey, your favorite jam, or thick wedges of Brie.

This recipe is also suited for your breadmaker. Place all ingredients into the pan in the order given. Use the setting for 1 1/2 pound, whole wheat bread with a dark crust.

The stuff that calls young Johnnies to an opportune floor meeting with their favorite Benedictine Brother or Father so they can cram it into their faces weighed down and oozing with butter, honey, and peanut butter and jelly. The stuff that calls students to the Reefer (a.k.a. The Refectory) morning, noon, and night to be loaded with ham, bacon, turkey, roast beef, American cheese, Swiss cheese, cheddar cheese, tomatoes, onions, lettuce, mayonnaise, and anything else that fits in a 5-by-5-inch area. The stuff that calls alumni and visitors to the Great Hall after a football victory or a tour of the Abbey Church. Like Johnnies call Bennies for "help with homework," Johnny bread calls us for nourishment.

More importantly, it calls us to recognize the hard work and self-sustainability by a group of Benedictine men who set out in the mid-1800s to build a center for worship and study in dedication to God. It calls us to remember the sweat on an old monk's brow and his calloused hands from working in the fields and cutting firewood to heat the ovens. In an age where too often we forget about the amenities we have, where technology and convenience take the place of social development and contemplation, Johnny bread calls us back to humanity. It calls us all to sit down for a moment together so we can appreciate the human community that we all are and to give thanks for what we have. Johnny bread calls us together.

Fritz Ebinger

Biographies

Fr. Tim Backous, OSB is a monk of St. John's Abbey and long time Johnny bread addict. He hails from South Dakota and now serves as the Assistant Athletic Director at St. John's University as well as working in Residential Life and Institutional Advancement.

Bryan Bohlman, 2002, is currently a student at St. John's University majoring in history. From nearby Richmond, Minnesota, he has been a member of the student senate, played varsity football for the Johnnies from 1997 to 2001, and he was a proud employee of the St. Ben's Writing Center for three years.

Judy Dodge is a former Bennie, sister of the author, biochemist/epidemiologist, singer, professor at Chesapeake Bible College and Seminary, and co-owner of Petrini Shipyard and Marina in Annapolis, Maryland. Currently she lives in Maryland.

Fritz Ebinger, class of 2001, graduated from St. John's with a B.A. in philosophy. He is currently working as a Peace Corps volunteer in the premaculture sector with subsistence farmers and youth in Veraguas, Panama.

Al Eisele is editor of *The Hill*, a weekly newspaper covering Congress that he helped start in the summer of 1994. He was been involved in journalism, government, academia, and business for nearly four decades. He served as a press secretary to Vice President Hubert Humphrey and former senator Eugene McCarthy. A native of Blue Earth, Minnesota, he is a graduate of St. John's University. He served as a commissioned officer in the U.S. Army and was a pitcher in the Cleveland Indians baseball organization. He and his wife, Moira, have two children.

Don Hall, born in St. Cloud of lumbering people, then schooled at St. John's for high school and some college, then Marquette University, after which he worked for forty years, some time at Control Data, but most recently as a stockbroker until the end of the century collapse, lives in Minneapolis.

Lee Hanley, a Faribault native, graduated from St. John's University in 1958 and refused to go home. Over thirty-eight years, he built a career around teaching, photography, editing, publications, proposal development, and taking notes for his memoirs. Along the way, he spent six years working in Washington and has the distinction of having worked for every Olson who has ever served in the U.S. Congress. He retired in 1997 and lives with his dog in Walker, Minnesota.

Shaun Johnson was born and raised in north central Iowa; he was a tutor in the CSB Writing Center, graduated from St. John's, and is presently a member of the internationally touring a cappella group, Tonic Sol-Fa.

Eugene J. McCarthy was born in Watkins, Minnesota, in 1916 and graduated from St. John's University in 1935. After a short teaching career, he entered politics where he has spend most of his life: in the U.S. House of Representatives (1949 to 1959) and in the U.S. Senate (1959 to 1971). His run for the presidency in 1968 was instrumental in bringing an end to the war in Vietnam. He lives in Virginia now where he writes. McCarthy is also a great storyteller, especially about the sandlot baseball days in central Minnesota where he was a key player.

Richard Nicolai grew up on homemade bread that his mother baked daily, graduated from St. John's in 1958, and immediately began teaching high school English and humanities in Austin, Minnesota, and continued to do so for more than thirty years. He has also been an adjunct instructor at the local community college. He and his wife, Pat, are both retired teachers who enjoy traveling whenever possible, especially to visit their children who live in the far reaches of the U.S.

Roger Nierengarten graduated from St. John's after returning from World War II. He practices law in St. Cloud where he lives with his wife, Dee.

Cyril Paul graduated from St. John's in 1959 with a BA in English. He was born in Desros, Trinidad, West Indies. Presently, he works from his home as an artist in residence and a musician. His hobbies are jogging, cycling, and poetry writing. He recently completed the Heartland AIDS Ride from St. Paul to Chicago.

Ryan Poindexter, SJU 2000, BS Biology, spent his years in college learning about monkeys, trying to become a great American writer, and searching for secret tunnels under the campus. He began a trek through Asia after graduating and now two years later is still on the go. He is currently living in western Japan, teaching English. He finds the bread in Japan not nearly as tasty or satisfying as Johnny bread but will stick around long enough to learn the secrets of rice farming.

Lawrence Poston, MD, graduated from St. Cloud Cathedral High School and started at St. John's in 1953. He left for three years to serve in the U.S. Army and then returned to finish in 1959. He graduated from medical school at the University of Minnesota in 1963. He practiced in Caledonia, Minnesota, until 1986. He then taught family practice for the medical school until 2002, when he retired. He married Vera Thelen of Waite Park, Minnesota, in 1960. They have five children and eight grandchildren.

James Rickman is a New Mexico native who has spent far too much time hanging around Los Alamos, New Mexico, the birthplace of the atomic bomb. He earned a degree in philosophy from New Mexico State University and now earns a living writing about science for Los Alamos National Laboratory. He has served on the Los Alamos County Council, he enjoys atomic folklore, and is an accomplished blues harmonica player and chess aficionado. This is his first published limerick.

Robert Shafer graduated from St. John's in 1956. He worked on Capitol Hill for Representative Alvin O'Konski and left to become vice president at Pfizer Pharmaceutical Company. He lives in Rye, New York, with his wife, Ellen.

Andrew Sjodin was born in Pipestone, Minnesota, in 1981 to a dad named Paul and a mom named Charlotte and has a sister Ameigh. He attended Forest Lake schools, was on the swim team for six years, earned the Eagle Scout award for the Boy Scouts of America, and graduated with honors in 2000. He currently is a student at St. John's majoring in philosophy. He is a member of the St. John's swim team. Andy likes to eat, hunt, play ping pong, and hang out with his best buddy, Buck, a Weimaraner

Fr. Hilary Thimmesh, OSB, joined Saint John's Abbey in 1947, began teaching English in 1956, completed doctoral work in English at Cornell University in 1963, and has held administrative positions from time to time, including presidency of Saint John's University from 1982 to 1991. His mind is peopled by writers and saints and Civil War generals—notably Julian of Norwich, her contemporary, Geoffrey Chaucer, William Shakespeare (who he believes wrote Shakespeare's plays), and Ulysses S. Grant for his modesty and good writing.

Catherine Rae Derry Wallace graduated from the College of St. Benedict in 2002. She worked as a tutor in the CSB Writing Center under Elizabeth Stoltz's expertise and felt privileged to be a part of the cookbook project. Currently, she is a graphic artist at three local newspapers based in St. Joseph, Minnesota. She hopes one day to write and publish a book of her own.

Eileen Derry Wallace of New London, Minnesota, is the mother of the photographer of this cookbook and an oblate of St. Benedict, St. John's Abbey.

George Wacek is the proud father of Jen Wacek, former tutor at the CSB Writing Center and soon-to-be teacher.

Martin Wera, SJU 2000, BA Spanish, served the last two years as an Americorps member, first in Portland, Oregon, with Portland Habitat for Humanity as Assistant Site Supervisor, and then in Washington, D.C., as an Employment Counselor at Neighbors' Consejo, a bilingual, social service provider in northwest D.C. He co-led a service trip to Miramar, Costa Rica. Currently he is beginning graduate work at the Humphrey Institute at the University of Minnesota studying for a Master's degree in Public Policy.

Epilogue

You are now witness to the vast range of uses stale Johnny bread has. There was one more use that doesn't appear in the book, suggested by a friend, Shelly Brandl, and followed through by my sister Judy. It was a recipe using bread crumbs mixed with cement and sand to form a flower planter. I tried it: it cracked and smelled so bad, I threw it out. But that idea gave rise to a series of other uses of Johnny bread, expressed in verse, beginning with my frustration and then my sister joining in with a St. Ben's perspective. The room on the next page is for your own versions of Johnny bread whether in the kitchen or in a verse.

A cook who had lost inspiration,
Knit her brow in dark consternation
I'm tired of this bread,
So I'll use it instead
In the walls for my home's insulation.

"I'm in bed and I must get well faster,
So what shall I do?" he then ask'd her.
"I'll soak Johnny bread
In beer for your head,
In lieu of your mother's mud plaster."

In spring from the winter we suffer;
Our roads just get rougher and rougher.
The pot holes need fill;
This bread fills the bill:
Its bulk an appropriate buffer.

At the wedding of friends Dave and Betty
All was prepared and quite ready.
"One thing's missing," guests said.
"We'll use Johnny bread,
All in crumbs for the farewell confetti."

EAS

The plaster used meal of the corn,
A Bennie art teacher showed scorn.
She crumbled the bread,
Used its remains instead
And the Johnny bread planter was born.

The gravel pit's closed, so no bread,
The refectory notice once read:
An action impeded,
A substitute needed:
The La drowned her sorrows instead

Judy Dodge

66

Notes and Ideas